Copyright©2016
Library of Congress Registration Number: 2016952122
ISBN 978-0-9864405-4-0
By: Charity S. Snyder
Printed in the United States of America
All rights reserved to the Author, Charity S. Snyder

No part of this publication may be reproduced, stored in a retrieval system, or transmitted in any form or by any means – electronic, mechanical, photocopying, recording, or otherwise- without the written permission of the publisher and copyright owner.

Published By: Azaida Media, LLC
  7726 Gunston Plaza #1648
  Lorton, VA 22199
  www.azaidamedia.com

Poetry of Adoption

My Struggle to be Triumphant

DEDICATION

To my lovely parents,
William and Cynthia Snyder,
You have loved and cared for me
despite everything.

To my sister, Ara Snyder,
who always talks to me and does
some of the things that mom does
such as doing my hair.

To my church family,
the lunch brunch crew,
Aunt Lee, Aunt Brenda, and
Pastor White and family.
Thank you for always
being there to support me.

To my birth parents,
for releasing me to
bigger and better things
so that I could accomplish
things such as this.
I love you all!
Thank you and
GOD bless.

Table of Contents

Questions & Consequences.................... 1
    Who Are You
    Why
    Have You Ever
    Sixteen
    Time

Deep Hurt................................... 9
    I Cry
    Games
    Letting Go
    Adopted
    Stuck
    Joke
    Struggle
    Long Gone
    It's Too Hard
    Trust Me
    Left Behind

Self Esteem 23
    I'm Fake
    The Real Me
    Book
    Dear Mom and Dad
    Bad Girl
    My Problem With Life
    The Stuff You Can't See
    Low Self-Esteem
    Me

Table of Contents

Bullied 39
    Disrespected
    Being Told
    Trapped

Struggle With Love. 45
    Love
    Take or Give
    Forbidden Love
    Break Up
    Disguised Trust
    Will You Cry With Me?
    Love Is

Light 55
    Trying
    Changing
    Someone Special
    With Wings I Can Fly
    I Am Undefeated
    A New Me
    Our Creator

Hope 65
    I Tried
    It's Okay
    Transforming
    Growing Up
    Hope
    Dreams

Introduction

I am Charity S. Snyder, also known as Tatyana. My journey in writing began when I was 13 years old, and it has evolved as a tool for helping me cope with some of life's challenges. I was adopted when I was very young. Since coming of age, it has often bothered me that my birth parents decided to give me away. As a result, I found myself constantly battling with emotional issues.

I started writing because I found it to be therapeutic for me. Writing has helped me release the pain and hurt that many adoptees face. It can be difficult trying to process why your mother would give you up, why she did not want you, or why you were labeled a mistake. And although those questions may never be answered, I still have hope in finding my birth parents some day.

Many of my writings were done while I was in a residential treatment facility. I had been dealing with a lot of issues, and I looked for anything to help relieve the pain I felt on the inside. So, having been inspired by Maya Angelou, Emily Dickinson, Terry McMillan, Nikki Giovanni, Langston Hughes and James Baldwin, I turned to writing as a means to release my innermost feelings and help calm my spirit.

I hope that everyone who reads this book will follow their dreams and become all that they desire to be. I also hope that it will help others who may be struggling with some of the same issues as I have. Thank you for taking the time to read my poems, and I hope that you enjoy them!

Poetry of Adoption

Questions
and
Consequences

Poetry of Adoption

WHO ARE YOU

Who are you deep down inside
Crying for help, I see it in your eyes.

Who are you and what do you want to be
You don't have many goals from what I see.

Who are you disrespecting others,
cursing everyone out because you're mad at
your mother.

Who are you to tell me what I can't be
You're not going to bring me down like I'm
blind and can't see.

Who are you to lie about yourself,
knowing every day, you really need some help.

Who are you to walk around this world,
thinking you're number one but headed for a
downward spiral.

Who are you?
From what I see, is a person who needs to be
rescued from living in a dream.

WHY

Why does there have to be so much hatred?
Why does this world have to be so destructive?
Why do we have to live with so much pain?
Why are children not eating?
Why are so many people dying?

Why aren't enough people trying to make a change?
Why do people have to experience things beyond their control?
Why are we letting the world bring us down?
Why is this happening to my family?
Why is this happening to me?

These are questions we ask ourselves every day.
At the end of the day, we have to ask ourselves, "Why do we keep asking why?"
None of our questions can be answered until we ask ourselves, why?

HAVE YOU EVER

Have you ever wanted to dry a tear that you knew you made fall?
Have you ever said some things that you never meant at all?
Have you ever wanted to reach out to someone who was in pain?
Have you ever wanted to give sunshine to someone who lives in the rain?
Have you ever wanted a chance to go back and change the past?
Have you ever stopped to realize that time slips by too fast?
Have you ever loved someone and never told them so?
Have you ever held back a question that you really wanted to know?
Have you ever felt you might explode from holding stuff inside?
If so, that's when you make a choice between happiness and pride.

SIXTEEN

I'm so excited. I'm finally sixteen.
I got my license and feel really free.
My mom kisses me bye and tells me to be safe,
I say, "I'll be fine", and kiss the side of her face.
I then go to a party, and there I only drink sprite
I have a great time with friends before calling it
a night.

In route on my way home, I'm happy and
driving fine;
But a drunkard runs the light, and hits me
in the side.

> *Mom, I promise I was driving safe,*
> *but I guess I was something he didn't see.*
> *I know you're sad, but be strong for dad.*
> *I was daddy's little girl and I was his world.*
> *Put "daddy's little girl" on my grave, and*
> *keep momma's little angel in your heart.*
> *You'll see me soon enough,*
> *so don't be too sad.*
> *I'm looking upon you every day,*
> *until you come with me to stay.*

TIME

I spend all my time trying to get people to like me, and it never pays off.
People tell me I should stop wasting my time and open my eyes.
Time.

My parents spend all their time trying to help me, and I never let them.
Time is wasted on people and lots of material things.
Time.

The time goes by way too fast.
When it finally slows down, you're out of time.
You want it to speed up again but it doesn't.
You wish you could have that time all over again to do bigger and better things.
But it's all over, time is up.
Time.

Poetry of Adoption

Deep Hurt

Poetry of Adoption

I CRY!

Every time I see your face, I cry.

You said you loved me, I cry.

Then you lied, I cry.

Abandoned by my blood family, I cry.

Bound by pain, I'll break the chain, I cry.

X's and O's, hugs and kisses, I cry.

You raised me, you loved me,

and you've always cared, I cry.

No matter what, you are my family, I cry.

DNA doesn't make a family, love does, I cry.

GAMES

Sometimes I think it's all a game,
but really I'm just ashamed of my name.
No, I'm ashamed of my ways.

By days, I try and try to lie; and I really just
want to die; but I can't.

I have to stay alive and thrive to do my very best
in life, even though it's hard.

I have to keep myself from yards, yards of
people who only bring me down.

I'm around; around for a reason, a season,
a season of games.

Poetry of Adoption

LETTING GO

My past is over, my adoption is over.

My birth mom is gone, my past is gone.

It's so hard to let go.

Everyone tells me that letting go

is good for my heart.

I don't think they understand how bad I feel.

Letting go will only make me angrier,

to know that my questions can't be answered.

Well if you think I'm letting go, you're wrong.

Sometimes I just can't.

Letting go is just not going to work for me;

however I will gladly try.

ADOPTED

Mom, Dad.

Adopted.

Who knew?

One day I'll meet you.

Guess how much I grew?

Waiting to see the truth,

But I don't want to.

I just want you!

Adopted.

Mom, Dad I love you.

STUCK

I'm stuck in my ways
by discomfort and pain,
asking when my days will end.

The longer I stay, the more I pay.
None of these problems will go away.

I'm asking you to please
help me through the night,
because you know I think I'm right.

I'm stuck just trying to get to the light;
praying that someday I'll be alright.

Charity S. Snyder

JOKE

I feel mad.

I feel sad.

I feel glad.

No, that's dumb.

Glad is a feeling I've never had.

Give that thanks to my birth mom and dad.

Ha! What a joke!

They left their daughter behind,

hoping that I'd go crazy.

Good thing that wasn't the case.

Surprise to them, I'm winning the race.

STRUGGLE

We struggle.

We struggle in a battle of tears and pain.

All we feel is hurt, and all we see is rain.

We struggle with the joy of the blessed life.

We are trying to find our path.

We struggle trying to figure out the basic needs of life.

We struggle seeing the pain of others.

We have to know every step to be taken.

We struggle more and more and more…

LONG GONE

As I lie here in my bed,
I think about what was once said.
A dream so bold and true, it's different for me
than for you.

My dreams died long ago; and truth be told,
I don't care no matter what words roll.
I don't share my goals or feelings,
for they have shriveled up and died;
and I sit here and I cry.

I look back at my childhood, when told my
dreams were dumb.
I stood up for what I believed in and wanted,
as I moved to the beat of my own drum.

I was still a kid with hopes and dreams and a
spirit so bright.
But now I lay here in the middle of the night,
hoping and believing that my good night dreams
will finally come true.

IT'S TOO HARD

When you are asked to do something,
do you ever say it's too hard or I can't?
Well as for me, I know whenever I say that
it means that I don't want to.

Can you shred these things for me, Charity?
It's too hard.
Clean up your room, Charity.
It's too hard.
Get up, Charity. It's time to go to school.
It's too hard. I'm tired.
Clean up your mess at the table, Charity.
It's too hard.

Well, that is my excuse for everything.
It's too hard is a phrase some say when they
simply don't want to do something.

So, next time you want to make an excuse
to avoid doing something you don't want to do;
think about the fact that quickly getting it done
allows you to move to something fun.

It's too hard just doesn't cut it.

TRUST ME

Every time I do something wrong,
I try to turn it around so that you can trust me.

You let me do things, but I don't do them right.
I just want you to trust me.

Everything you do and say is for a reason,
but I don't believe it.
I just want you to trust me.

I now realize that I have to do what you want
me to do, in order for you to trust me.

I'm on my own and have not a clue what to do.
If only I would've done what you told me to do.

LEFT BEHIND!

Every night I close my eyes
hoping it will be alright.

Left behind.

My dreams somewhere far away,
I want to take the pain away.

Left behind.

Wide awake and always on guard,
for you never know when you'll have to run.

Left behind.

When I ponder on all that happened as a child,
 I realize that I was left behind.

Poetry of Adoption

Self Esteem

I'M FAKE

I'm fake.

Can't you see?

I'm fake.

Not showing the real me.

I'm fake.

I lie through my teeth.

I'm fake.

I say what I need.

I'm fake.

I mean it, it's no lie.

I'm fake.

It's so bad, I want to cry.

I'm fake.

I want to state my truth.

I'm fake.

I just don't know what to do.

I'm fake.

Can you help me, please?

I'm fake.

THE REAL ME

I'm scared to show you the real me, scared to
know what you'll see. I bring heartache and pain
like a gloomy day when it rains. I'm scared to
know what you'll see, when I show you the real
me.

The real me who I know,
 I'm really still afraid to show.
It's not pretty, in fact it hurts and it's depressing.

It feels the worst to show you the real me,
but I must be brave to reveal what you'll see.
So I'll take off part of my mask
and reveal only my top layer;
because the deeper I go, the scarier it gets.

Honestly, I don't know if you're ready to see it.
It hurts to know that I have lied;
it hurts so badly, I want to cry.

I've not been honest with myself
nor those around me.
Although I have been real to a degree.

I've hidden the anger and depression for awhile,
and now I can't take it anymore.
It suffocates me, you see;
to not show you the real me.

I feel it closing in around me,
and it tears me apart.
But now, I feel I can show you a part of me
that I hope you're not afraid to see.

If I take off my mask
and tell you why I put it on,
I'll be forced to look inside;
and then I'm sure I'll want to cry.

BOOK

Like a book.

I am like a book.

I have many secrets.

If you look at my cover,

all you will see is a bold faced lie.

I hide my true beauty,

my true being,

and who I really am.

Without my cover,

all I would do is die.

Poetry of Adoption

DEAR MOM AND DAD

I can't stand to live anymore. I just want to die
and end it all. The pain of living is just the start,
I'm sorry that I'm breaking your heart.

It started with hate, but now it's a little too late.
My life is a mess; and I can only confess that
inside, it hurts none the less.

I'm sorry for all the trouble I've caused; but in
the end, it will be okay because this is the only
way. I'm sorry for worrying you. I'm sorry for
distressing you.

I'm sorry for killing you inside.
Mom it saddens me to see you cry.
You're the one who has helped me get by.
You taught me to walk, you taught me to talk.
Without you, I wouldn't even be here,
and I will always hold you dear.

Dad, you're the greatest guy in the world. I've
never appreciated the times we've had.
Inside I was always a daddy's girl, but I never
showed you that I cared.

Without your guidance I wouldn't be here, as
you've always told me I had nothing to fear.
For such a long time I have felt this way,
and all I have to say is…"I love you".

Somehow that doesn't quite seem like enough;
because I know that all you've gone through
at times has been really tough.
You are the best parents a girl could ever have.

BAD GIRL

I steal. I lie. I cut. I run.

I'm such a bad girl they all say.

Do they really know how I feel?

The world has me thinking that what I do

is the most horrible thing in the world.

I do it because it's the only thing I know to do.

I tell myself that I'm a bad girl.

I'm just so bad.

But the truth of the matter is, I'm not bad.

I just make bad decisions.

No matter what people say, I and the world

will always view me as the bad girl.

MY PROBLEM WITH LIFE

They all say you're never promised tomorrow;
but never said anything about pain and sorrow.

One day I'm smiling and have no problems.
The next day I'm fighting back my tears, and
asking who will solve them.

Why give me tomorrow if I didn't ask for it?
I'd rather have a chance in life, and not have to
deal with my emotional issues.

I sometimes feel as though life is something I
want to forget.
When will it all get better?
When will I find success?
But they all just say I'm not trying my best.

Poetry of Adoption

THE STUFF YOU CAN'T SEE

A war rages inside me.
Emotions against emotions,
thoughts against thoughts,
One has to come out on top.

Weapons are drawn, aimed and fired.
I stand somewhere in the middle
helpless, scared and tired.

I try to gain control, but I'm pushed away.
My energy to fight is instantly drained.
I want to scream for help; but when
I open my mouth, nothing comes out.

I watch in horror as thoughts and emotions
are shut down and destroyed.
Stray bullets keep hitting me,
but there's nowhere to run.
I want to give up, but that's not a choice.

On the outside, I appear calm and collective;
letting no one see, what's going on inside me.

LOW SELF-ESTEEM

I'm not good enough.
I have an ugly face.
I'm not pretty.
No one likes me.
I'm not smart.

This is what people like me think about themselves every day. It's called low self-esteem. I have it; and some of you reading this just might have it.

It brings you down. It makes you think that you're not good enough…but you are.
Don't let what other people say affect you, because God made you just the way he wanted to; and you're valuable in his eyes.

I have made a great change, and I want you to do it too. Every day, look at yourself in the mirror and say, "God loves me and that's all that matters."

I love myself. Will you love you?
Don't let low self-esteem bring you down!

ME

Me

I want to be free
of the pain and hurt I see.
Tell me now if we should be
taking this life seriously.

Me

I'm scared to be
the person you wish to see.
Right now it's hard to accept reality.

Me

I'm asking you to please let me be;
I can't seem to embrace
this thing called dignity

Me

Poetry of Adoption

Bullied

Poetry of Adoption

DISRESPECTED

I'm disrespected every hour, every minute, and every second of every day.

People want me to treat them with dignity and respect. Why should I?

You can't even stop talking for one minute
to let me say my peace.
So should I be respectful?
I think to myself…No!

Tell me one good reason why I should treat you
nice. Perhaps it is because I am a nice person,
or it is the right thing to do.
So, I just bite my tongue and walk away.

Although they keep saying stuff;
I just let it roll off my back.
I tell myself it will be okay in the morning.

But when I wake up and go to school,
I just get disrespected all over again.

Now I am ready.
I have been praying.
All I have to do is ignore them and let God take care of the rest.

Well guess what? It stopped!
It turns out that they actually liked me.

BEING TOLD

Some have told me that
I'm not going to make it.
Well guess what? I kind of believe it.
I've been to hell and back
trying to figure out how to break it.
How do I break the cycle
of partly believing everything I've been told?
You're too old; you're too young.
You're not smart; you will never win.
Well, I've never won.

Fake it to make it is what they say.
Sometimes it's harder to see the bigger picture
when everyone else only sees you failing.
I try to tell myself it will be over soon,
or until one day I get told it's over.
I've had my chance and there's no going back.

Now it's the end…the end of my life? NO!
It's the end of class and time for the next.
I don't know what will happen.
Some have told me that I won't make it.
Well guess what? I don't believe it!

TRAPPED

All this time, I have been trapped;
trapped in my emotions and thoughts.
I wish they would let go of me.
I don't want them anymore.
I just want to be normal.
I'm trapped though.

I tell people that I have been dealing with
emotional issues since I was 9 years old;
and they are still present.
I've been in and out of hospitals;
in and out of residential treatment facilities.
Nowhere to go. I'm trapped.

This time I say that I will break the chain.
I will conquer my emotional issues.
I will stop fighting against my help.
Maybe, just maybe,
this time I won't remain trapped.

Poetry of Adoption

Struggling

With Love

LOVE

Love is overrated.

Love is something

that we all wish we had.

When we receive it,

we don't stop and think that

it is not only a necessity…it is a feeling.

It only dies when it is given,

but no longer accepted.

We have to open up

our hearts and receive.

It may take some time,

but we will learn how to love.

TAKE OR GIVE

A girl living on her own,

skin black,

she's skinny and tall.

Her insecurities take over;

so sometimes she has trouble

expressing how she feels.

Every time she tries,

she gets put down.

She gives her all to people

who in turn give nothing.

It's only take or give.

FORBIDDEN LOVE

It's funny how you can love someone who
doesn't love you back.
Forbidden love.

You think that you have found the one, but he
doesn't even know you are there.
Forbidden love.

Your lips touch his and it's the world to you,
but he doesn't even blink an eye.
Forbidden love.

Your eyes meet and everything just goes away,
but it all comes back when he says it's nothing.
Forbidden love.

Finally, you come to your senses and realize
that he is not even aware that you like him.
Everything that people have told you
begins to make sense.
Now, you truly know that it is forbidden love.

BREAK UP

You said you loved me, but you lied.

So I did what I could to say good bye.

You said you'd never leave, but you lied.

I did my best to go along for the ride.

I ran away to hide because you altered my pride.

I loved you unconditionally,

but I guess it just wasn't meant to be.

And now I sit here and I cry,

over all of the things that I tried.

Even though this is not a bribe,

I still have my heart set on you and I.

DISGUISED TRUST

They tell me they're just here to help me;
but they don't listen to me when I speak.
Yet they want to hear me when I don't.

They tell me they understand me;
but when I ask for help,
they don't know how to help me.

They say they know what's best for me;
but they want to send me back to the place
where I was miserable.

They get irritated when I'm depressed,
yet suspicious when I'm happy.

They get mad when I tell the truth,
but seem satisfied when I lie.

They want me to trust them.
They want me to spill my secrets at their feet.
I have my reasons for believing what I believe,
and for trusting who I trust.

We all have our reasons.

WILL YOU CRY WITH ME?

You have to lie to live,

and smile to get through the pain.

If they see that you are weak,

you will no longer live, but exist.

You must hate me,

but I've done nothing wrong.

Why did you hurt me?

I don't know why I smile

at the pain you caused me?

I won't cry, but will you?

LOVE IS

Love is letting go and never looking back.

Love is beginning a new chapter in one's life.

Love is sharing yourself with the one you care about the most.

Sharing yourself is the telling of secrets; the things you would not even tell your dearest friends.

Because this person is in your life, you are not afraid to speak.

Love is listening to their problems and their accomplishments.

Love is a give and take.

Love is a team effort with each giving and taking one hundred percent.

Love cannot be spoken, for it is one's heart.

Love is a feeling that is hard to explain;
it is an understanding between two that is not always spoken, but felt.

Love is everlasting and empowering;
it can seize everyone in its path and uplift them.

Love is amazing.

Poetry of Adoption

Light

TRYING

I'm really tired of trying;
trying to be perfect for everyone
that comes my way.

I'm actually trying this time around.
I'm trying to make a change.

How am I supposed to do well this time if I'm
too scared to be me?
I'm tired of trying to be someone that I'm not.
If I blow my cover, then I won't be trying.

I'm giving in; giving in to the pressure and the
madness of this hard and sacred life.
So what do I do? I stop trying, and then wait a
few days and try again.

What happens when you fail? Is it all over?
Do you actually stop trying? NO!
You get back up, try and try, and keep trying!

"If at first you don't succeed,
Try, try, try again."
- William Edward Hickson

CHANGING

have to change my outlook on life.

I have to listen to my mother

just because she's right.

Even though I have no more might,

I have to keep pushing on

until I've won the fight.

Even though right now

it may be night,

my father always told me to

never let go of the light.

SOMEONE SPECIAL

I know someone who is special.
This person has changed my life
in more ways than can be said.
He has taught me to be myself.
He has loved me just for me.
He has made me a more loving person.
He has shown me the difference
between right and wrong.
He has cared about me
more than words can express.
He is a friend to me and anyone else
who cares for and about him.
You may wonder, "who is this person?"
Why of course He is my Lord and Savior, Jesus.
He died to set me free, and for that,
I am so very thankful to Him.

WITH WINGS I CAN FLY

I glide over whispers of wind, going around every rivers bend. Moving over enchanting valleys of flowers, as I float above the oceans, I feel all of its deep powers.

I will ride the wind through the rain. I feel the laughter; there is no pain. I will move in and out of each waterfall. I will do flips with the sparrows, and I will chirp and sing with the blue birds.

As I fall in love with the sky and think of not a thing; I have no worries, no place to go but through the wind. Where I will end up nobody knows. I sing a new song of the sky. I pass the streets as I go by. I see my friends and family while the wind is beneath my wings.

I fly way up high into the night sky. I play with the moon and the stars, all I feel is warmth. I imagine my body without scars. Wild horses running swiftly beneath me; I think this is so glorious, how can this be? With wings I can fly, so let me be.

I AM UNDEFEATED

I am undefeated!
Beaten
Lied to
Hated
Laughed at
I've had a lot done and said to me
Yet, I'm still here.

I'm still standing,
tall and proud;
and I will not fall.
I will hold my ground.
I will stand proud
until they lay my body down.

I will win this war we call life.
I can.
NO!
I will do it.
Because I am UNDEFEATABLE!

A NEW ME

So many times I tell myself
I'm going to change.
I say, this time it's going to be different.
Well this time it is.

I went to a facility to get help
with my emotional issues.
At first I was reluctant.
Then, I opened up and let them help me.

I feel better, I feel new.
A new me.
I'm ready to start over.
This time it's going to be different.
A new beginning…a new me.

OUR CREATOR

You created us.

You created this world.

You created nature.

You are powerful in all that you do.

Who can heal us like you do?

Who can work miracles like you do?

No one can but my creator, God almighty.

I am special.

Even when I don't feel like I am special,

I know that I am because God created me!

Poetry of Adoption

Hope

I TRIED

I tried to give up on my parents.
I tried to give up on myself.
I tried to give up on life;
but it didn't work.
It never works.

I tried to give up on time.
I tried to give up on beauty.
I tried to give up on wanting to be me;
but it didn't work.
It never works.

So, one day I decided
that I will try to do better.
I try to stop the negative thoughts.
I try to say everything will be okay.
I've tried and I will keep trying;
even if I must get help.

Charity S. Snyder

IT'S OKAY

I can't pretend to know how you're feeling.
I know that I have issues.
I know the problems I constantly battle.
I know the scars of what I have been through.
I was abandoned by my birth mom.
I was not protected in foster care.

Regardless, what happened to me
will always remain part of my past.
I must learn to accept what I cannot change.
Maybe one day, I will be able to
forgive and forget.

As for now, I must realize that
I did nothing wrong.
No matter how I feel,
I must believe that I'm okay.
It's all okay.

TRANSFORMING

I've lied.
I've stolen.
I've cried.
I've told.
I've snuck around.
Now I'm bound to walk this earth
and live a life of sorrow and pain,
and of heartache and vain.
I'm trying to change.
I'm trying to fix me.
I'm trying to care,
but it's just so hard.
I'm use to the hostility of hate.
I'm use to the hurt and pain.
But being here, I know I'm going to change.
Not for anyone other than me.
Can't you see?
I'm transforming.
I'm a better person and my progress is amazing.
I can't wait to show you the different me.

Charity S. Snyder

GROWING UP

As I have been growing up,
I have been through a lot.
I have learned a lot.

As I have been growing up,
I have experienced a lot of problems.
Growing up, I have taught myself
to shutout the pain.
I told myself to never let anyone in.

Growing up, so many people
have tried to help me;
but I refuse to let them.
Growing up, my parents always told me
that I can be helped. I just have to let them.

Growing up has been a great struggle.
Growing up, I'm learning not
to let my emotions overtake me.
Growing up is tough, but I will make it through.

HOPE

I hope.

Hope that one day I will be normal.

Hope that I won't have to deal

with the pain I feel.

Hope that I will make it to heaven.

Hope that I will see my birth parents one day.

Hope that I learn to allow people to help me,

instead of shutting them out.

We all can have hope.

But will we? That is the question.

I hope that I will wake up the next morning.

Do you have hope?

DREAMS

Dreams are the things that keep you going.

When you feel like a failure,

they keep on flowing.

Dreams are the torch that lights your heart.

When everyone else stumbles,

you still know your part.

Dreams are a window to the future;

They bring you hope on a bad day.

They are always there to help you cope.

Never let your dreams go without a trace,

or you may find yourself losing the race.